THE
OCEAN
BOOK

STUDY GUIDE
& WORKBOOK

For more information, write:
Answers in Genesis, PO Box 510, Hebron, KY 41048

Printed in the United States of America

www.AnswersInGenesis.org

Contents

Answer Key available at
    www.answersingenesis.org/cec/guides.asp

Introduction

Terms to Know and Spell

Locations of the various oceans and seas

Short Answer

1. The oceans cover _____% of the earth's surface area and contain _____% of all the surface water on the planet.

2. How do the oceans protect the earth?

3. How do the oceans provide both food and oxygen for mankind?

4. What are some of the sources of power in the ocean?

5. About how much of the current production of oil and petroleum comes from the ocean?

6. The oceans have been used throughout history as a means of _____; this is one of the reasons that three-fourths of the American population lives within _____ miles of a seacoast.

7. List what contributes to the color variations of seawater:

   blue

   yellow

   green

   brown

Discussion Questions

1. How might life on Earth be different if the oceans were larger or smaller than they are now?

2. Why should we care about what lives in the oceans when we can only live on land?

3. Should one country have a say in how another country cares for its neighboring marine habitats? Give examples to explain your answer.

Activity

1. On a blank map of the world, label:

Arctic Ocean	Atlantic Ocean	Indian Ocean
Pacific Ocean	Arabian Sea	Bay of Bengal
Bering Sea	Caribbean Sea	Coral Sea
East China Sea	Greenland Sea	Great Barrier Reef
Gulf of Mexico	Labrador Sea	Mediterranean Sea
North Sea	Norwegian Sea	Philippine Sea
Red Sea	Scotia Sea	Sea of Japan
Sea of Okhotsk	South China Sea	Weddell Sea

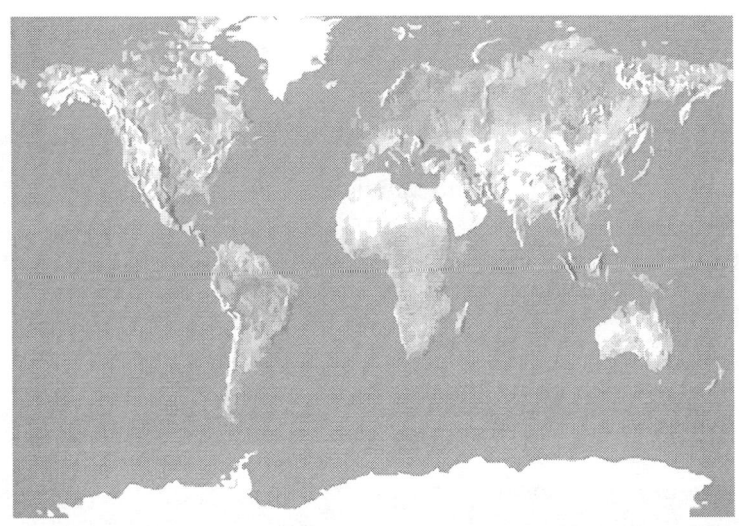

1

Research and the Deep Oceans

Terms to Know and Spell

ability to transmit sound and light

acidity of sea water

air-sea interaction

animal and plant life

biological oceanography

chemical and physical changes

chemical composition of sea water

chemical cycles

chemical oceanography

currents

density

food webs

interaction of life with its surroundings

marine geology and geophysics

nature of dissolved gases and solids

oceanic sediments and rocks

physical oceanography

properties of magnetism, gravity, electricity, heat flow and
    seismic methods

sea ice

temperature

tides

waves

Short Answer

1. What are the four major branches of oceanography, and
    how are they differentiated?

2. Name seven human endeavors that benefit from
    knowledge of oceanography.

3. How was the Challenger expedition able to disprove
    Professor Edward Forbes's theory?

4. Name two other discoveries made by the Challenger.

5. What is a seismic profile?

6. In what ways have exploration methods changed since
    the 1990s?

Discussion Questions

1. Compare the attitudes of Earth's citizens toward the ocean 50 to 100 years ago with attitudes in the 21ˢᵗ century.

2. Discuss the human endeavors that benefit from knowledge of oceanography in greater depth.

Activities

1. Memorize and recite Psalm 107:23–31.

2. Prepare an outline as shown. Complete the outline, using the letters to represent the four branches of oceanography listed in the terms above, and the numbers to categorize the sub-topics for each.

   I. Branches of Oceanography

   A.

       1.

       2.

       3.

       4.

   B.

       1.

       2.

       3.

       4.

5.

6.

7.

8.

C.

    1.

    2.

    3.

    4.

D.

    1.

    2.

Projects to Do on Your Own

Rewrite Psalm 107:23–31, paraphrased in your own words.

Choose one branch of oceanography that interests you. Do 1–3 hours of research on the subject and jot down some notes. Turn in a one-page reflection on what you learned to your teacher, or discuss the principles with family or classmates.

2

Physical Characteristics of the Ocean

Terms to Know and Spell

abyssal plain

beach

brackish water

coast

continental margin

estuary

harbor

hydrothermal vent

inlet

lagoon

oceanic ridges

salinity

salt marsh

seamount

shoreline

subduction

trench

Short Answer

1. What are five major geo-physical features of the ocean? (Choose your answers from the list above.)

2. Define and/or illustrate the other terms listed above.

3. Explain what forces cause coastlines to differ in appearance.

4. What difference(s) exist between a fjord and a lagoon?

5. What are the parts of the continental margin?

6. Trenches, oceanic ridges and hydrothermal vents are all part of the _____ _____.

7. Contrast trenches with oceanic ridges.

8. Describe the compound word "hydrothermal" in terms of its parts, and tell how these combine to define the term.

9. Compare the temperature of water from a hydrothermal vent to the temperature of the water boiling in a pan on the stove.

10. Describe three creatures that thrive near hydrothermal vents.

Discussion Questions

1. Describe guyots and seamounts in terms of their appearance. How or why is each one thus shaped?

2. What formed the trenches in the ocean floor?

3. Tell how the geological activity in Iceland or the hostile environments of deep-sea hydrothermal vents can be used to support the biblical view of special creation.

4. What principles should town councils and residents in eastern America's coastal cities consider in constructing edifices along the coast?

Activities

1. This chapter is full of fascinating trivia. Divide into groups of 2–3, and copy interesting statements, leaving out a key word. Conduct a "sea bee," much like a spelling bee, and see who can remember the most information.

2. Discuss what physical features or forces cause coastlines to differ in appearance.

3. Gather information from news media or the internet about beach cities affected by erosion or suddenly changing coastlines.

4. Study the Pacific Ocean on a globe to locate the island arcs and other formations described on p. 14.

Projects to Do on Your Own

1. Use papier-mâché, play dough or modeling clay to construct a model showing the five major physical characteristics of the ocean floor. When dry, label each of the features with a letter (A–E). On a sheet of paper, make a key to your model which names each of your features and gives a brief description of each.

2. Research and find out if Juan de Fuca Strait, which lies between the Olympic peninsula of Washington State and Vancouver Island, British Columbia, Canada, is formed by the Juan de Fuca Ridge.

3
Composition of the Oceans' Waters

Terms to Know and Spell

commodity

dehydration

desalination plant

pinnacle iceberg

salinity

tabular iceberg

Short Answer

1. What are the most common elements of seawater?

2. Since every 1,000 grams of ocean water contains 35 grams of salt, what percentage of seawater is salt?

3. Where does the salt in seawater come from?

4. Why is it dangerous for humans to drink seawater?

5. Why is seawater not of uniform salinity all over the world?

6. What is an iceberg?

7. Only ____% of an iceberg can be seen above water; ____% of its bulk threatens because it is hidden below.

8. Most pinnacle icebergs are formed in the _____. Tabular icebergs break off ice sheets formed near the _____.

9. Why is April 14–15, 1912, considered as one of the most disastrous events in maritime history?

Discussion Questions

1. Define and review each of the terms on the previous page.

2. Discuss how the answer to #8 above helps to explain what caused the Titanic tragedy.

3. Consider why salt was such an important commodity in history. Then consider Jesus' words in Matthew 5:13. Why do you think Christ compared His followers to salt?

Activities

1. Memorize and recite Matthew 5:13.

2. Use an etymological (word origins) dictionary to find the origin of the word "salary." What did you learn about the importance of salt throughout history that would explain what the words "not worth his salt" or "salary" means in today's culture?

3. Float an ice cube in a clear glass or measuring cup. Using a centimeter ruler, measure how much of the ice cube protrudes above the water's surface and how much extends below. Compare your data to the 10%/90% ratio of icebergs. Would you expect results to be the same? Why or why not?

Projects to Do on Your Own

1. Try rubbing a small piece of raw meat with a lot of salt. Will this simple procedure allow the meat to dry without rotting? (Be very careful when handling raw meat. Be sure to wash your hands after you're finished!)

2. Research how submarines and aircraft carrier crews are able to furnish a large number of soldiers with fresh water, while they are at sea for extended periods. Construct a model of a desalination plant or experiment with a simplified evaporation system.

3. Do research to locate the various "salt flats" of the world. Which countries produce and/or export the most salt?

4. Find out which oceans are the least salty and the most salty.

4

Tides, Waves and Currents

Terms to Know and Spell

centripetal acceleration

Coriolis effect

current

diurnal/semidiurnal

gravitational pull

gyre

landmass

neap

neap tide

nutrient upswelling

oscillate

quadrature

revolve/revolution

riptide

spring tide

surf

syzygy

tide

tsunami

undertow

wave

Short Answer

1. The rising and falling of the level of the ocean near a shore is called the _____.

2. What affects the amount of surf along a coastline?

3. The force of gravity can be described as the measurable and descriptive function of the mass of the objects involved and ___ _____ _____ _____.

4. Who was the first scientist to apply the law of gravitational forces to the predictable nature of the tides?

5. Syzygy occurs when the sun, moon, and earth all line up in a row, which results in very high or very low _____ tides.

6. When the positions of the sun, moon and earth form a ninety-degree angle, _____ tides occur. This _____ causes the lowest _____ and the _____ ____.

7. _____-_____ tides form two high tides and two low tides each day.

8. Most waves are formed by _____ _____.

9. What factors influence the amount of surf along a beach on a particular day?

10. A _____, or tidal wave, is a devastating, giant-sized wave caused by _____ _____.

11. What do the red or blue arrows on a map of ocean currents mean?

12. What are the most famous ocean currents for North and South Americans?

Discussion Questions

1. Why is it important that seafarers be aware of the tides?

2. What kind of person is compared to waves? Read James 1:5–8 and discuss its implications.

3. Role-play tides, currents, quadrature and syzygy. Choose one student to "stir" invisible water up and down in a vertical circle. Position another student nearby who will stir the water around and around in horizontal fashion. Select two more students to act the part of the sun and the moon and position them in alignment or at 90-degree angles to the "currents." The currents should lean closer to the moon and the sun as directed, to model the gravitational effects on the tides.

Activities

1. Memorize and recite James 1:5–8.

2. Locate "no tide" Tahiti and the infamous high-tide Bay of Fundy on a map or globe. Have various students discuss their personal (humorous) experiences with tides or surf.

3. Define each of the terms listed on pages 20–21.

4. Divide the class into 3 groups: the waves, the tides and the currents. Have students write questions or true/false trivia statements pertaining to their subject area. Conduct a "sea-bee," much like a spelling bee, or "whirl-pool" like a knowledge bowl, and see who can remember the most information. Celebrate the success of the winner by doing a group "wave" cheer.

Projects to Do on Your Own

1. Research the life and writings of Sir Isaac Newton. Find out if he was a creation scientist because it was the fashion of the day, because scientific observation supported his conclusions or because of some other matter.

2. Construct an artificial beach with clay, sand and water in a large pan and experiment with the force and motion of waves.

3. Study the diagram and explanation of the tides on page 24. Gather balls of various sizes and use them to symbolize the gravitational forces on the tides at the various positions. If possible, use a digital camera to record the sequence. Share the images with classmate(s) as you describe the tidal terminology.

5

Weather

Terms to Know and Spell

Coriolis effect

density

depression

El Niño

eye of a hurricane

hurricane

hypothermia

La Niña

meteorology; meteorological

storm surge

thermocline

tropical storm

Short Answer

1. Devastating Hurricane Andrew pummeled _____ with winds gusting up to 177 mph in August 1992.

2. _____ is a warm water current which appears around Christmastime off the coast of Peru.

3. List two to four effects of El Niño.

4. _____ is a seasonal cold-water current that keeps phytoplankton from growing, and many marine creatures starve due to a lack of nutrients.

5. At the equator, the earth turns at a rate of approximately _____ mph.

6. Since the earth spins to the _____, waters tend to accumulate at the _____ shores of the continents.

7. An area of warm air with low pressure over a large body of water is called a _____.

8. A tropical depression with winds greater than 50 mph is called a _____.

9. A hurricane is rated as a category 1 to 4 storm based on its _____.

10. A hurricane in the Indian Ocean is called a _____.

11. A hurricane in the South China Sea is called a _____.

12. Due to the Coriolis effect, hurricane winds spin (clockwise/counterclockwise) in the Northern Hemisphere and (clockwise/counterclockwise) in the Southern Hemisphere.

13. Why do hurricanes become so strong in the open sea?

14. Out of about 50 tropical depressions, only ____ or _____ become hurricanes.

15. Water heats and cools more _____ than land does.

16. The _____ is an area of increasingly cold water that reaches from the surface zone down to about half a mile below sea level.

Discussion Questions

1. Reread the sections on the Coriolis effect (page 36) and ocean currents (pages 27–30). Then read historical accounts of the age of explorers, circa 1450–1850. Discuss how the two scientific principles may have affected human history.

2. Compare and contrast the times, locations, causes and effects of El Niño and La Niña weather phenomena.

3. If a hurricane carries 100+mph winds, why does it only travel 25–35 miles per hour, unlike a tornado which gives almost no "escape" time?

4. Ask students who have weathered a hurricane to retell their experiences. Then conduct a discussion as to what various people's responses should be toward preparedness and cleanup (i.e., a home builder, a property owner, a parent, a businessman, a law enforcement officer, etc.).

Activities

1. Memorize and recite Matthew 7:24–27.

2. Prepare a small hurricane pinwheel and label it with the name and date of the most devastating hurricanes of the last century. Plot the pinwheels on a map to show where major hurricanes have struck coastlines on North America or Asia.

Projects to Do on Your Own

1. Obtain and study a week-long series of weather maps or satellite photos. Find high-pressure areas and low-pressure areas. Does the air in the high-pressure area move directly to the low-pressure area? Why or why not?

2. If a hurricane is currently developing somewhere in the ocean, obtain several satellite photos that show its progression. See if you can predict its precise landfall before it is reported by newscasters.

6

Harvesting the Ocean

Terms to Know and Spell

shellfish

trawling

purse seining

dredging

overfishing

bykill

Short Answer

1. Most of the ocean's living creatures are found in the upper ___ feet of the sea.

2. Name at least two different small, medium and large fish, and some shellfish harvested from the ocean.

3. What happens to caught fish that are not used for food?

4. How has modern equipment and technology helped fishermen?

5. What is overfishing and what does it mean?

6. What is an "aquaculture" farm, and what is produced there?

7. Name three of the most abundant "crops" from mariculture.

8. Put the following terms in order of their importance in producing energy from the ocean: tides, salinity, thermal gradients, currents, waves.

9. Although thermal gradients are capable of producing enormous amounts of energy, why aren't more power plants being built?

10. What nonliving resources are also harvested from the sea?

Discussion Questions

1. From 1950 to 1990, the world fish catch increased from 20 million tons to more than 90 million tons. Discuss whether or not this increase can continue, and the implications of overfishing. Should fishing restrictions be imposed and enforced? If so, by whom?

2. What are some ways that overfishing can be prevented?

3. Discuss the benefits and detractions of offshore oil or gas production.

Activities

1. Memorize and recite Luke 5:3–7a, the great draught of fish.

2. Form small groups to learn more about fishing techniques, such as dredging, drift netting, gill netting, longlining, purse seining and trapping. Research the purpose, equipment, method and product of the technique, as well as statistics on the amount of marine produce harvested (in tons). Share your data with the class.

3. Research and discuss the fishing production from the Grand Banks by decade over the last hundred years. How have changes in fishing affected the lives of area residents?

Projects to Do on Your Own

1. What kinds of fish or shellfish are sold at your local supermarket? Do research to determine how they are harvested and brought to market.

2. Learn more about how hydroelectricity is produced from tidal power.

3. Find out why manganese nodules are so valuable.

7
Marine Life

Terms to Know and Spell

algae

aquatic mammals

benthic zone

bioluminescence

bony fish

cartilaginous fish

cephalopod

crustacean

gastropod

horizontal zone

intertidal zone

kelp

midnight zone

mollusk

neritic zone

oceanic zone

pelagic zone

phytoplankton

plankton

red tide

sunlit zone

twilight zone

vertical zone

zooplankton

Short Answer

1. Why do most living marine organisms inhabit the sunlit zone?

2. Why is an abundance of plankton so vital to marine biology?

3. What are the major differences between phytoplankton and zooplankton?

4. What is a kelp forest?

5. Name and describe the four kinds of marine algae.

6. Lobsters and spiders are both arthropods. What do lobsters have that spiders do not have?

7. How are fish classified?

8. What are chordates?

9. How might you tell which classification a certain fish may be if you cannot see its skeleton?

10. Why does the natural behavior of barnacles irritate seamen?

11. Give an example of a food chain.

12. Compare a food chain to a food web.

13. Study the photo of the blackdevil anglerfish on page 55. What special designs did God give this creature to ensure its survival?

Discussion Questions

1. Although many more creatures inhabit warmer waters (phytoplankton), diatoms are abundant in coldwater regions. How could this be one of God's special provisions for Arctic or Antarctic ecosystems? Can your answer help to refute evolutionary ideas?

2. How can a jawless fish eat if it has no jaws?

3. How are whales like fish? How are they different from fish?

4. What does the fossil record reveal concerning the origin of fish?

Activities

1. Make a mural with pictures of commonly harvested marine life.

2. Memorize and recite Genesis 1:20–22.

3. On a large map, label the various productive fishing areas of the world. If possible, list the types of fish

harvested from each area and the fishing techniques employed.

4. If you live near the coast, plan a field trip to a tidal pool, aquarium or other marine park. If possible, have students touch the invertebrates found in a tidal pool.

Projects to Do on Your Own

1. Purchase, prepare and taste some of the varieties of fish available for human consumption.

2. Read the labels on pet food and yard fertilizers to see if they contain marine products.

3. Some sharks look like bony fish. Research the swimming and "breathing" capabilities of sharks and bony fishes to discover identifying behaviors.

4. Do further reading on recent research concerning whale migration patterns and use of echolocation.

8

Exploring the Coral Reef

Terms to Know and Spell

atoll

barrier reef

coral bleaching

equatorial region

fringing reef

Great Barrier Reef

mangrove

polyp

shoal

Short Answer

1. Some of the marine invertebrates that inhabit a coral reef include _____ _____.

2. Sinking underwater volcanoes formed _____ and _____ reefs.

3. Masses of dead coral skeletons harden and turn into _____.

4. A jellylike creature that will grow into a mature coral is called a _____.

5. An underwater extinct volcano sank and the circle-shaped coral reef that encloses it is called a(n) _____ _____.

6. How did the Great Barrier Reef get its name?

Discussion Questions

1. Define each of the terms in the list above.

2. Tell how a coral polyp is like a plant and like an animal.

3. Give several examples to describe how particular characteristics of a mangrove tree helps tropical habitats to flourish.

4. Why are coral reefs dangerous to ships?

5. Tell how does the coral growth rate measured in 1997 helps to refute evolutionary uniformitarianism and support the special creation model of origins.

Activities

1. If you live near the coast, plan a field trip to a salt marsh, intertidal zone or marine park; or have experienced students describe their experiences with snorkeling or diving in the sea.

2. If you live in a "land-locked" state, contact a local pet store to find the location of the nearest saltwater aquarium. If possible, obtain a specimen of a living coral or sea anemone for students to observe. An alternative would be to view a documentary on an underwater excursion at a coral reef.

3. There are many different kinds and colors of coral. Have groups or individual students study geographic regions to determine which areas sport various types of coral and pertinent reef formations. If possible, make a wall chart to compare and contrast the type of reef, type of coral, pattern of growth and examples of other life supported by the coral reef. A good place to start is with popular tourism spots that advertise snorkeling or scuba diving.

Projects to Do on Your Own

1. Research your local library for more information about the types of fish that inhabit coral reefs. Where do they live? What do they eat? Why are they suited for living among coral?

2. Search the internet for photos and information about atolls, fringing reefs and barrier reefs, as well as the forms of life dwelling there. Compile a scrapbook with pictures and captions. Include pertinent labels regarding geographic locations.

3. Plan a trip to a major aquarium or tropical reef. Popular tourist attractions include the Hawaiian Islands, Bermuda and the Virgin Islands. Some major US cities such as San Diego, San Francisco, Denver, Orlando and New Orleans have marine parks or aquariums.

4. Further develop your computer technology skills and design a tri-fold travel brochure to a luxurious location near a coral reef. Include tantalizing descriptions and visuals of a snorkeling expedition to the reef.

9

Oceanic Vessels

Terms to Know and Spell

Archimedes principle

ballast

displace

diving plane

hull

mid-water drifter

oceanographic research ships

Polynesia

submersible

Short Answer

1. A _____ is any device that can successfully venture into the deep and return to the surface carrying information about the underwater world.

2. What kinds of equipment can be found on most submersibles?

3. Prepare a chart from a large sheet of butcher paper or newsprint that lists all of the submersibles named in the list of terms below. Then list the purpose or mission for each one and the particular equipment used. Tell whether it is manned or remotely operated. If possible, include a picture example of each.

diving bell	bathysphere	bathyscaph
DSV	ROV	DSRV
submarine		

4. How does a bathysphere differ from a bathyscape?

5. What is a Nansen bottle?

6. Why aren't nuclear submarines used more frequently during peace times?

7. What was the Trieste?

8. The study of liquids and the forces of pressure is called _____.

9. Archimedes principle states that the force holding a vessel in water is _____ to the _____ of the fluid being displaced (pushed out of the way).

Discussion Questions

1. How have advances in technology improved marine research techniques in the last 70 years?

2. How does a submarine dive and surface?

3. Submersibles, oceanic research vessels and submarines are very costly to construct, use and maintain. Is oceanic research really worth it?

Activities

1. Memorize and recite Psalm 139:9–10.

2. Obtain articles, with photos, of various kinds of submersibles. Have students write summary paragraphs about special features (capabilities) and pertinent information obtained in research expeditions.

3. View a documentary film or video on oceanographic research by Jacques Cousteau, or interview a USS sailor who has served aboard a submarine.

4. Have small groups of students experiment with the Archimedes principle with objects of various sizes and shapes. If desired, used calibrated containers and measure the weight of water displaced.

Projects to Do on Your Own

1. Read the book *Kon-Tiki* by Thor Heyerdahl to learn about this man's determination to sail across the Pacific Ocean in a balsa wood craft.

2. Contact a personal acquaintance or Navy recruiter to learn about the particular training or preparation needed to live and work on a submarine for extended tours at sea.

3. Visit a dry dock area at a seaport. Study the size of the ships and the shapes of their hulls. Notice the color variations painted on the sides of a ship, indicating fill-weight limitations. If possible, observe a ship being loaded and setting out to sea. Consider how the Archimedes Principle applies to these ocean-going vessels.

10
The Genesis Flood

Terms to Know and Spell

dimensions

hydraulic

sedimentation

Halocline diagram

density gradient

Mount St. Helens

submarine canyon

uniformitarianism

sediment gravity flows

cichlid fish

Cambrian

Short Answer

1. _____ ___ was designed by God to withstand the ravages of the Genesis Flood.

2. What verses show the Flood was worldwide?

3. Recently scientists discovered evidence of "water roaring out of an overfilled lake [that] carved an instant Grand Canyon" not on Earth, but on the planet _____.

4. What is the name of the diagram that shows the density gradient between salt and fresh water?

5. Massive underwater avalanches are also called?

6. In one day of geologic activity in 1982, a 1/40 scale model of Grand Canyon was formed where?

7. According to Genesis 7 and 8, the Flood lasted ____ year(s).

Discussion Questions

1. Is it logical to assume that massive layers of sediment found, for example, spread across the United States, are due to slow processes over millions of years of time (uniformitarianism)? Would a catastrophic event (i.e., a flood) better explain what is found—such as the St. Peter sandstone described on page 71?

2. If one were to reinterpret the biblical teaching of a worldwide flood to that of only a local event, what would this do to interpreting other important doctrines in Scripture?

3. Why did God send the Flood?

Activities

1. Memorize and recite Genesis 7:21–22.

2. Prepare a drawing of Noah's Ark on a large sheet of paper. Use the principle of ratios to determine the approximate size of the Ark compared to people and animals such as horses and cows. How many doors would you put on the Ark? Why?

Projects to Do on Your Own

1. Look up the 2002 article of a grand canyon on Mars by Paul Recer. After doing some cross-referencing in different publications, write a report of this amazing geological event on the Red Planet.

2. Research the Mount St. Helens eruptions of 1980 and 1982. Although the sediments laid down were of volcanic origin, scientists know the thousands of layers were clearly formed over a short time period. See if you can find pictures of these sediment layers. Do they look like the layers of sediment found at the Grand Canyon?